Copyright © 2024 Irina Chasov
All rights reserved.

No part of this publication may be reproduced, distributed, or transmitted in any form or by any means, including photocopying, recording, or other electronic or mechanical methods without the prior written permission of the publisher, except as permitted by U.S. copyright law.
For permission requests, contact irina.chasovart@gmail.com

Library of Congress Control Number: 2024911737

ISBN: 979-8-9908950-0-3 (Hardcover)
ISBN: 979-8-9908950-1-0 (Paperback)
ISBN: 979-8-9908950-2-7 (ebook)

Editing, Cover Design, and Illustration by Irina Chasov.

For information about special discounts available for bulk purchases, sales promotions, fund-raising, and educational needs, contact via email at irina.chasovart@gmail.com

www.irinachasov.art

First printing edition 2024
Printed in the United States of America

To Miron.
Your smile brightens every room
and your attention to detail
inspires me every day.

Athlete Apple

Bb Ballerina Bow

Bicycle   Books

Cc

Cape

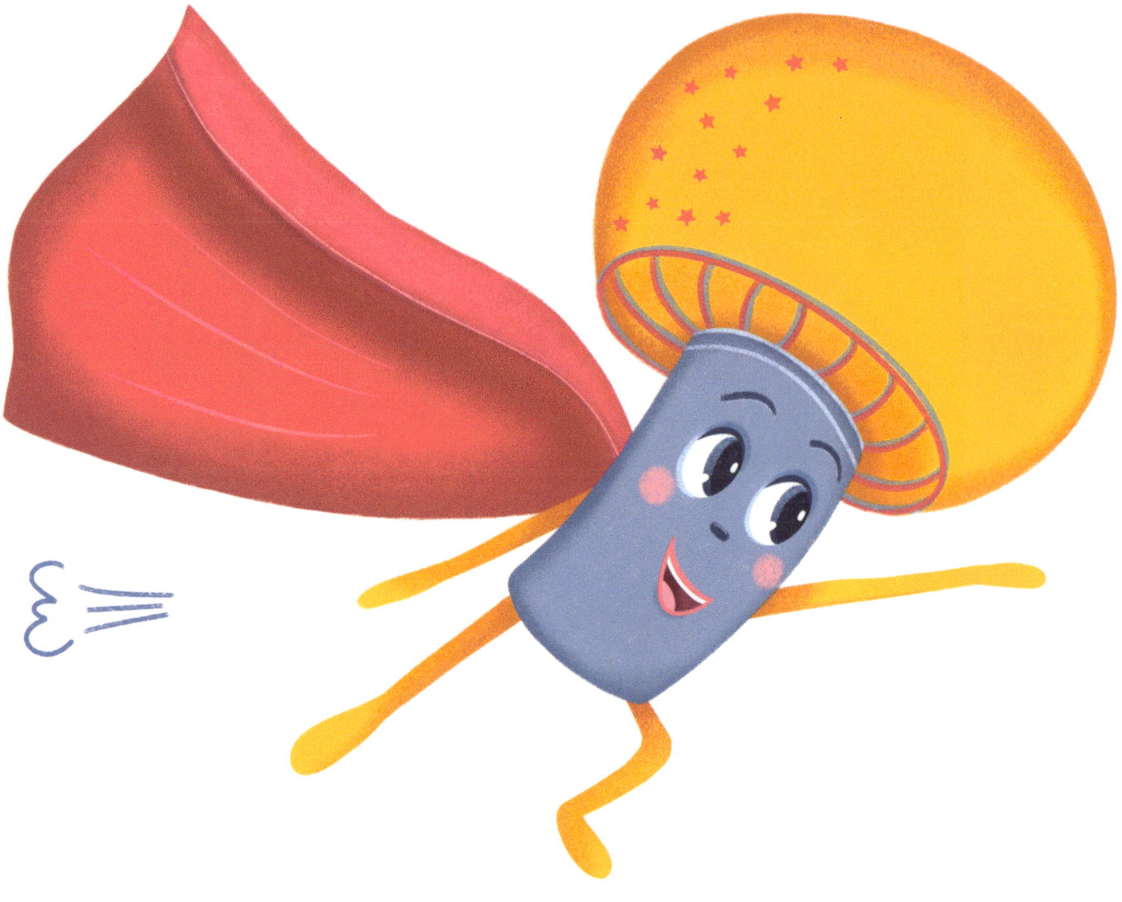

Courage

Cook
Cake

yummy

Dd

Dancers　　　Daisy

Ee

Engineer

Ff

Fairy
Frog

Florist Flowers

Grandparents Gecko

Grandma

Hh

Honey Farmer

Investigator Iguana

Ii

Jj Jump rope

Kite

Ll

Love
Lovender

Mm

Mother

Rr

Robot
Rainbow

Scientist Ss

Tt

Tent
Telescope

Umbrella U u

Vv Violet Valentine

Ww

Woodchuck

Xx

X-ray

Yogi   Yy

breathe in ★   breathe out ★

Zz Zoologist

Aa Bb Cc Dd Ee Ff Gg Hh Ii Jj Kk Ll Mm Nn Oo

Pp Qq Rr Ss Tt Uu Vv Ww Xx Yy Zz

Teaching kids the alphabet can be a fun and engaging process. Here are some tips to help make learning the alphabet enjoyable and effective:

1. Use Visuals and Colors: Bright, colorful alphabet charts, flashcards, and books can capture a child's attention and make learning more engaging.

2. Hands-On Activities: Encourage kids to form letters using playdough, trace letters in sand or rice, or use finger paints to write letters.

3. Letter of the Week: Focus on one letter each week, incorporating it into various activities and learning sessions.

4. Label Objects: Label items around the house with their corresponding letters to help kids make connections between letters and words.

5. Positive Reinforcement: Celebrate successes and progress with praise and rewards to keep kids motivated.

6. Consistency: Regular, short practice sessions are more effective than occasional long ones. Aim for daily practice to reinforce learning.

7. Storytelling and Role Play: Create stories and role-play scenarios that involve using letters and words.

By incorporating these tips, learning the alphabet can become a fun and integral part of a child's daily routine.

How to use this book:

1. Point and Identify: As you read, point to each letter and its corresponding picture. Encourage the child to repeat the letter and the name of the picture after you.

2. Discuss Each Page: Spend time discussing each page, asking questions about the pictures, and encouraging the child to describe what they see.

3. Interactive Questions: Ask interactive questions like, "Can you find the B on this page?" or "What other words do you know that start with C?"

4. Repetition: Read the alphabet book multiple times. Repetition helps reinforce learning and makes the child more familiar with the letters.

5. Relate to Real Life: Relate the letters and pictures in the book to real-life objects and experiences. For instance, after reading "S" for Scientist," talk about who scientists are.

6. Follow the Child's Interest: If the child shows particular interest in certain letters or pages, spend extra time exploring those together.

7. Praise and Encourage: Offer positive reinforcement and encouragement to build the child's confidence and enthusiasm for learning.

Hi, my name is Irina.
I am a self-taught artist who has always been drawn to the magic of illustration. From the moment I turned the pages of my first picture book, I was captivated by the power of storytelling.

Now, as an illustrator, I have the privilege of giving visual life to the characters, landscapes, and adventures that ignite the imaginations of young readers around the world.

When I am not lost in the world of illustration, you can find me exploring nature's wonders, savoring a cup of coffee with a well-loved book, or dreaming up new illustrations to share with the world.

www.ingramcontent.com/pod-product-compliance
Lightning Source LLC
Chambersburg PA
CBHW040724060526

44119CB00083B/318